Animal Family Albums

Dogs

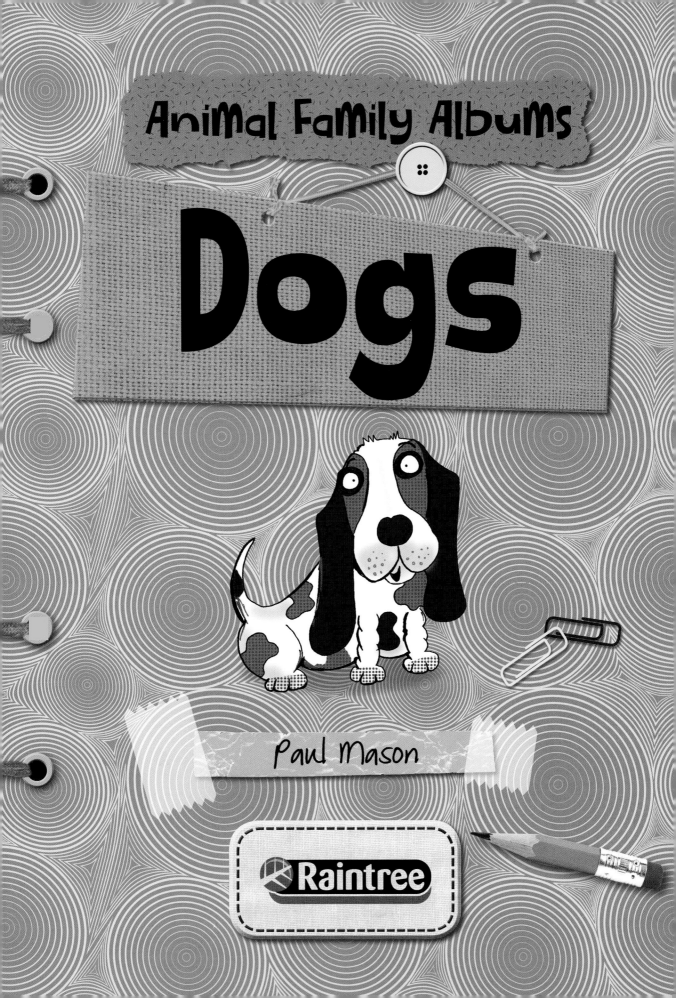

Paul Mason

Raintree

Raintree is an imprint of Capstone Global Library
Limited, a company incorporated in England and Wales
having its registered office at 7 Pilgrim Street, London,
EC4V 6LB – Registered company number: 6695582

To contact Raintree:
Phone: 0845 6044371
Fax: + 44 (0) 1865 312263
Email: myorders@raintreepublishers.co.uk
Outside the UK please telephone +44 1865 312262.

Text © Capstone Global Library Limited 2013
First published in hardback in 2013
The moral rights of the proprietor have been asserted.

Edited by Nancy Dickmann and Laura Knowles
Designed by Philippa Jenkins
Original illustrations © Clare Elsom
Illustrations by Clare Elsom
Picture research by Liz Alexander
Originated by Capstone Global Library Ltd
Printed and bound in China by CTPS

ISBN 978 1 406 24957 6 (hardback)
16 15 14 13 12
10 9 8 7 6 5 4 3 2 1

British Library Cataloguing in Publication Data
Mason, Paul, 1967-
Dogs. -- (Animal family albums)
636.7-dc23
A full catalogue record for this book is available from
the British Library.

Acknowledgements
We would like to thank the following for permission
to reproduce photographs: Alamy pp. 13 (© Charles
Mistral), 16 (© David Cole), 26 (© Graham Franks);
Getty Images p. 27 (Jupiterimages/Brand X Pictures);
Nature Picture Library pp. 6 (© Bruce Davidson),
23 (© Bartussek / ARCO), 24 (© Edwin Giesbers);
Shutterstock pp. 4 (© cynoclub), 5 (© Marcel
Jancovic), 7 (© Gina Smith), 8 (© Eric Isselée),
9 (© Sergey Lavrentev), 11 (© Dale A Stork), 12
(© Mars Evis), 14 (© Shutter Lover), 17 (© Jagodka),
18 (© cynoclub), 19 (© photocell), 20 (© Daniel
Gale), 21 (© K. Kolygo), 22 (© Chris Kruger);
SuperStock pp. 10 (© Juniors), 15 (© Corbis),
25 (© Juniors).

Design elements reproduced with permission of
Shutterstock/© urfin (pencil); Shutterstock/
© Julia Ivantsova (pencil); Shutterstock/
© Studio DMM Photography, Designs & Art
(photo corners); Shutterstock/© wanchai (Blue
leather background); Shutterstock/© Sweet Lana
(blue pattern background).

Cover photographs of dogs reproduced with
permission of Shutterstock/© Erik Lam (bloodhound),
Shutterstock/© Jagodka (pug puppy), Shutterstock/
© Fesus Robert (hungarian Puli Dog), Shutterstock/
© Eric Isselée (Jack russell).

Every effort has been made to contact copyright
holders of material reproduced in this book. Any
omissions will be rectified in subsequent printings if
notice is given to the publisher.

All the Internet addresses (URLs) given in this book
were valid at the time of going to press. However, due
to the dynamic nature of the Internet, some addresses
may have changed, or sites may have changed or
ceased to exist since publication. While the author and
publisher regret any inconvenience this may cause
readers, no responsibility for any such changes can be
accepted by either the author or the publisher.

Contents

Some words are printed in bold, **like this**. You can find out what they mean by looking in the glossary.

Meet the family!

No one is sure how humans and wolves first began to live together. Perhaps extra-bold wolves came up to a campfire in search of scraps. Or perhaps humans found some wolf cubs and took them in.

Tame wolves turned out to be very useful. They warned if danger threatened the camp. They went hunting, helping to **track** and kill **prey**.

Whatever size or shape they are, every dog you ever meet is **descended** from wolves.

My name's Bob. I'll be introducing you to some of my family members. I myself am a Basset Hound. You can find out more about my **breed** on page 14.

Wolves and humans first began to work together more than 10,000 years ago.

Wolves became dogs

As time went by, the tamed wolves became less wolf-like. Some became smaller, and were good at catching rats. Others became slim and fast, and were good at chasing deer. The fiercest dogs were used for guard duty.

Today, some types of dog have become so specialized that they look similar to each other, and different from other types of dog. These are known as breeds. Dogs that are a mix of different breeds are called **mongrels**.

A dog's life

Some of my cousins still live in the wild. They never bathe, or even get a haircut! Even so, we pet dogs have a lot in common with them.

This pack of African hunting dogs is working together to track down its **prey**.

Food

Wild dogs and wolves eat meat. **Packs** of wolves **track** and kill large animals, such as moose. Smaller wild dogs eat rabbits, mice, and even birds. Like their wild cousins, pet dogs need a meat-based diet.

Living in a Pack

In the wild, dogs and wolves live in packs. The members do everything together, including hunting and eating. On cold nights, they huddle together in their **den** to keep warm. Pet dogs also like to be in a pack, and hate being left alone. Fortunately, dogs are happy to be in a pack made up of a human family – as long as they have plenty of company, they don't mind!

FAMILY SECRET

People say you can work out a dog's age in human years by multiplying its real age by seven. This is roughly true for big dogs, but multiply by five for smaller dogs.

Some dogs like nothing more than to curl up on a human's warm lap. Personally I prefer to be outdoors!

Pugs first appeared in China, hundreds of years ago. They became especially popular in a cold place called Tibet. The local **monks** sat with a Pug on their lap and tucked their hands under the dog for warmth.

Pug

Pugs are friendly little dogs that enjoy playing games as well as having a cuddle. Pugs have thick **coats**, and do not enjoy hot days. The folds of skin around their noses mean they wheeze a lot. Pugs also snore!

In French, papillon means "butterfly". The Papillon gets its name from the shape of its ears.

Papillon

It wouldn't be a surprise if Papillons were a bit snooty. After all, it was France's most famous king, Louis the Fourteenth, who first made the **breed** popular. King Louis liked Papillons because they are such clever little dogs. Papillons enjoy being trained and playing games – several times a day, if possible.

FAMILY SECRET

When Papillons first appeared, not all of them had ears that stood up. The ones with floppy ears became known as *phalene* – French for "moth".

Some members of my family just love to work. These dogs are full of energy. Their idea of a fun day out is herding sheep in the rain!

Pulis are unusual — but once you have seen one, you never forget its crazy coat!

Puli

Most Pulis have their thick **coats** knotted into cords by their owners. These thick knots mean drying a wet Puli is a long, tricky job! The Puli's **ancestors** stopped sheep from running away by jumping on the sheep and forcing them to roll on to their backs. Pulis bark a lot, and are very protective of their family. This means they make good guard dogs.

Border Collie

Don't get a Border collie unless you like long walks! These dogs are designed to run around herding sheep all day. A Border collie that has to stay indoors soon gets miserable. Border collies love learning new things, and they are fast and **agile**. They enjoy obedience classes, dog assault courses, and games.

FAMILY SECRET

One of the first Border collies was named Old Hemp. Old Hemp lived from 1893 to 1901. He was famous for being able to herd sheep by staring at them. His stare scared them into moving!

This Border collie is halfway round an assault course – and he's really enjoying it!

Water dogs

I'm not all that keen on swimming, but some of my cousins are. These two love charging into the water – even if it's really cold!

Labradors were bred to **retrieve** birds shot down over water.

Labrador Retriever

It's easy to see why Labradors are one of the most popular **breeds** of dog. They are friendly, playful, and easy to train. Labrador owners do need somewhere to dry off a wet dog, though. A Labrador's favourite game is running into water to fetch a ball or stick!

Portuguese Water Dog

As you might guess from their name, Portuguese Water Dogs love to swim! They originally worked on fishing boats. The dogs would fetch equipment that had been lost overboard, or carry things between boats. They could even herd fish into nets!

FAMILY SECRET

Portuguese Water Dogs are great at swimming, as you'd expect. What might surprise you is that they have webbed toes!

Portuguese Water Dogs became world famous when President Obama got one, called Bo, in 2009.

Time to meet a couple of the world's best sniffers! That's my own **breed**, the Basset Hound, and my great friend the Bloodhound.

Basset Hounds originally came from France. In French, *bas* means "low" — you can see how they got their name!

Basset Hound

If you enjoy running, you shouldn't get a Basset Hound – they can't move very fast! Bassets are friendly, good-natured dogs. They can be very stubborn and hard to train, though. The thing Basset Hounds like most is sniffing their way along, nose to the ground. Once a Basset Hound gets a **scent**, it will walk long distances trying to find the end of the trail.

Bloodhound

Bloodhounds are some of the friendliest dogs around. The biggest problem with bloodhounds is that they dribble a lot! Bloodhounds are famous for their amazing sense of smell. It is several million times better than a human's. Bloodhounds have used their noses to **track** down escaped prisoners and people lost in the wilderness.

FAMILY SECRET

Bloodhounds can identify people by their smell. In the past, some law courts even used to accept this identification as proof.

Bloodhounds can follow a scent left days before. One famous bloodhound, called Nick Carter, followed a scent that was ten days old.

Like me, these next two **breeds** love to take part in a hunt. Unlike me, though, they're also fast moving and full of energy!

Springer Spaniels get their name from their ability to scare out — or "spring" — birds for hunters to shoot.

English Springer Spaniel

Springer Spaniels were bred to run around all day. They would flush out **game** for hunters, or bring it back after it had been shot. This means they need lots of exercise. If you like long walks and throwing a ball to be brought back again and again, a Springer would be an ideal pet!

Pharaoh Hound

Pharaoh Hounds were once used for rabbit hunting. Hunters would send a ferret with a bell round its neck down the rabbit hole. The rabbit would run out – only to be grabbed by the waiting dog. Today, Pharaoh Hounds are usually kept as pets. They are good-natured and friendly, but they love to hunt. Never keep a Pharaoh Hound alongside pet gerbils, hamsters ... or rabbits!

FAMILY SECRET

When a Pharaoh Hound is excited, blood rushes to the dog's head, turning its nose and ears a glowing reddish colour!

Pharaoh Hounds are thought to have come from ancient Egypt.

Now it's time to meet some of the family toughs. These two were bred for **ratting**. They never back down from a scrap!

Many Jack Russell Terriers are **descended** from a dog called Trump, who was owned by a man named Jack Russell in the 1800s.

Jack Russell Terrier

You need a good fence if you have a Jack Russell. Otherwise it will escape and go exploring! The Jack Russell is one of the cleverest dogs around. Some even work out how to *climb* fences! Jack Russells are usually pleased to meet strangers, and play happily with children.

Fox terrier

Fox terriers have appeared in many films. For example, Tintin's dog, Snowy, is a fox terrier. Fox terriers are also fierce hunters of rats. If a fox terrier spots a rat, it grabs it by the back of the neck. Then it shakes the rat violently from side to side, which breaks the rat's neck. Fox terriers love their owners, but they can be a bit snooty towards other people or dogs.

FAMILY SECRET

There are two types of fox terrier: **wire-haired** and **smooth**. The photo below shows a dog with a wire-haired **coat**.

Fox terriers were bred mainly for hunting rats.

Some of my relatives just love the cold! It gives them a chance to get outside and rescue a human in distress.

Newfoundlands are tough, strong dogs. Their webbed feet help them swim well.

Newfoundland

Newfoundlands are amazingly strong. They were originally used on land and in the water. They could help gather in fishing nets, and even rescue drowning people. Today, some Newfoundlands are trained as lifeguards, and spend their time rescuing swimmers in trouble. Newfoundlands are sweet-natured, friendly dogs, and many are kept as pets. Watch out, though – their big, saggy mouths do mean that they dribble a lot and are messy eaters!

St Bernard

With their thick **coats** and digging skills, St Bernards were bred for rescuing travellers caught out in sudden snowstorms. They have an excellent sense of smell, and can even sniff out people buried by **avalanches**. The dogs lick people's faces to wake them. Then they lie beside them to provide warmth until help arrives.

FAMILY SECRET

One St Bernard, called Barry, is said to have saved the lives of at least 40 people. Barry lived in Switzerland between 1800 and 1814.

St Bernards have been rescuing humans in distress for hundreds of years.

The wild bunch

Some of my cousins still live in the wild. Sadly, they don't have very good manners – they would probably bite you if you tried to pat them.

The African hunting dog is sometimes called the "painted wolf".

African hunting dogs

African hunting dogs live in the grasslands and woodlands of Africa. Their big teeth and extremely powerful jaws easily crunch through bone. African hunting dogs hunt in **packs**. They work as a team, communicating with barks and yips. The dogs are almost three times more successful at hunting than lions. They mainly hunt antelope and young wildebeest.

This family of Australian dingoes is well-fed and happy — and like all cubs, these Dingoes are very playful.

Dingoes

Dingoes come from Australia. They are large, wolf-like dogs that live in packs. Dingoes do not always hunt together, and they are often seen alone. Their main **prey** includes kangaroos, **wallabies**, cows, rabbits, and rats. But dingoes will eat almost anything, from human rubbish to fish or insects!

FAMILY SECRET

Through the years, a few dingoes gave up the wild to live with humans. **Aboriginal Australians** have kept dingoes as pets for thousands of years. Today, some other Australians do the same.

Wolf pack!

Last of all, it's time to meet the original head of the family – the grey wolf.

These young wolves are play-fighting – practising for when they are fully grown.

Pack territory

Wolves live in **packs**. Each wolf pack has a **territory**, which it defends against other packs. Some wolf packs have giant territories. One pack in Alaska, USA, had a territory that measured 6,270 square kilometres (2,420 square miles). That's almost four times the size of London!

Wolves are amazingly strong for their size. A single wolf can turn over the frozen body of a horse or moose.

FAMILY SECRET

Wolves have lots of ways of communicating. These include making faces, body positions, marking objects with their smell, and all sorts of howls and growls.

Food and hunting

A wolf pack spends all its time moving around its territory, looking for **prey**. They prefer to kill and eat large animals such as moose or deer. Wolves will eat almost anything, though, including salmon, birds, and humans' rubbish. Although wolves are not usually dangerous to humans, they have been known to kill and eat people.

New dogs

Puppies are cute and cuddly, but they are hard work! Their owners have to do everything their mother would do in the wild. A puppy has to be fed several times a day. It must be kept warm and played with (that bit's easy!). And you have to clear up their wee and poo!

Most puppies arrive at their new home when they are just 8 to 10 weeks old.

Older dogs and mongrels

Adopting an older dog may be easier than getting a puppy. It will have learnt not to go to the toilet indoors! Also, giving a home to an older dog means it will not have to live in a cage at a rescue centre any more.

Many people prefer **mongrels** to dogs from a particular **breed**. Mongrels usually have fewer health problems, and live longer.

This family has decided to give a home to a dog that has been abandoned.

Everyone loves puppies, but they can be naughty! If you're like me and prefer a quiet life, a grown-up dog may make a better pet.

27

What type of dog are you?

You're not a dog, of course – you're a human. But dog and human personalities can seem quite similar. What kind of dog would your personality make you?

1. On a snowy day, what would be your idea of fun?

a) Stay indoors beside a warm fire and watch TV.

b) Go outside and start diving into snow banks, trying to discover what's hidden under the surface. There could be rats!

c) Play outside all day. And all night. And all the next day.

2. If someone suggests a team game, do you?

a) Agree to watch. As long as there's somewhere comfortable to sit, that is!

b) Insist that it's a game of chase. Ideally, chasing rats!

c) Phone the ice rink to book a court to play ice hockey.

3. Where do you prefer to sleep?

a) On a soft bed, with soft sheets and a hot water bottle, beside a radiator.

b) In a barn on straw – but you like to stay half awake in case any rats appear.

c) An igloo.

4. What's your favourite thing to eat?

a) Tasty snacks all through the day (they must be fed to you by hand!).

b) Rats! No just kidding, you don't actually eat rats. You'll eat whatever's put in front of you.

c) A warming meat stew.

5. Where would you prefer to live?

a) It has to be a palace, but I don't actually mind which country the palace is in.

b) New York or London – there are many rats there.

c) Iceland.

Answers

Mostly a: you like to be comfortable, warm, and well looked after – you are definitely a lap dog, such as a pug.

Mostly b: with your lively character and strange interest in rats, you would have to be a terrier, such as a Jack Russell.

Mostly c: no one who likes the cold as much as you could be anything but a rescue dog, perhaps a St Bernard.

Glossary

Aboriginal Australian person whose distant relatives were the first humans to live in Australia

agile able to move about quickly and easily

ancestor relative that lived long ago

avalanche slide of snow, rock, and ice down a mountainside

breed particular type of one kind of animal. For example, a Fox terrier is a particular breed of dog. All the members of a breed are a similar size and shape, and they look alike.

coat dog's hair, which covers its skin and keeps it warm

den place where a dog or pack of dogs sleeps and rests

descended related to an ancestor

game wild animals or birds that are hunted for food or sport

mongrel dog that is a mix of different breeds

monk person who spends his life living as part of a religious group or community

pack group of dogs or wolves, usually all related to each other

prey animal that is hunted and eaten by another animal

ratting catching and killing rats

retrieve bring something back. Retriever dogs were traditionally trained to bring back birds that had been shot down by hunters.

scent smell, or trail of smell, left behind

smooth with short hairs that lie flat against the dog's skin

territory area of land that an animal sees as its own space

track follow, using scent, sound, and other signs

wallaby small, kangaroo-like animal

wire-haired with longer hairs that are thick and wiry, with a rough appearance

Find out more

Books

Dogs (A Pet's Life), Anita Ganeri (Heinemann Library, 2009)

Poppy, The Dogs Trust Dog, Sophia Fergus (Hodder Children's Books, 2009)

The Ultimate Guide to Dog Breeds, Derek Hall (Lorenz Books, 2010)

The Usborne Little Book of Dogs and Puppies, Phillip Clarke (Usborne, 2009)

Websites

ukwct.org.uk
The UK Wolf Conservation Trust works throughout the world to help wild wolf populations. The site has information about the Trust's work in eastern Europe, Asia, and North America: look under the "Projects" tag.

www.rspca.org.uk/allaboutanimals/pets/dogs
The RSPCA website has lots of information about dogs and how to look after them.

www.ykc.org.uk
The Young Kennel Club is aimed at junior dog lovers. Its website has useful information on choosing, getting, and living with a dog.

Index